Ob

GW01007642

M

To Rita & Richard

An environmentally friendly book printed and bound in
England by www.printondemand-worldwide.com

X

FSC

Mixed Sources
Product group from well-managed
forests, and other controlled sources
www.fsc.org Cert no. TT-COC-002641
© 1996 Forest Stewardship Council

PEFC
PEFC/16-33-415

PEFC Certified

This product is
from sustainably
managed forests
and controlled
sources
www.pefc.org

This book is made entirely of chain-of-custody materials

1

www.fast-print.net/store.php

OBSERVATIONS
Copyright © Miriam King 2014

A catalogue record for this book is available from the
British Library

ISBN 978-178456-141-3

Contents

Like the fox 9

Of Soft White Nothingness 10

Bubble 12

Loneliness 13

What a Pity 14

The life of a bubble 15

Fog 16

The Green Homburg 18

This Is Your Driver Speaking 19

Thirty First Anniversary Walk ... 22

Without You 26

The Other Side 27

Forgotten in Time 28

'You're only young twice' 29

Every Now And Then 30

Early Morning 31

All the same 35

Ratty 38

1st Poetry Meeting 40

April Fool's Day 43

Fat Lip at Alton Waters	44
Last Time	46
Words	47
Incontinence Training	48
Emphysema	49
Employers	51
Oh Dear She's Cooking Again	52
To Pick Him Up	53
That First Smile	54
Leaving	55
Twelve Thirty	57
Even At Night	58
Just the way I am	59
What is the Matter With You All?	60
Such Futile Lives	61
Headmaster	62
Stream	63
Winning Through	64
Iris's Room	65
Invisibility	66
The Blue Floor	68
Chubby Laughter	69
Inebriation	70

Chance Meeting	71
The Beekeeper	72
Quintet	73
'Soufend'	74
When he took her hand	77
Middle age	78
Dreaming of Spring	79
Well You Know	80
Perfect Job	82
Physiotherapy	83
The Rebirth of Mankind	87
Flu	88
Nits and Lice	89
The Dell	92
Far Distant Valleys	93
No Right	94
Matron Greenslade	96
Childhood Beckons	97
The Chestnut Tree	98
Silken Threads	100
Half Forgotten Dreams	101
Romania	102
Alone	104

Will People Care	105
Travelling Companions	106
For Art's Sake	107
Post Natal Depression	108
A Witch's Spell For Winter	110
The Commode	111
Maggie	112
The Rape	113
The Abandoned Babies	114
Tuesday, 01 April 2014	115
The Circumcision	126
You Never Know	130
They Took Him	132
It's Pam Again Tomorrow	133
The Wait	134
Old Bill	135
Still the music	136
The Primitives	138
My Son's In Trouble	140
The Cigarette	142
Across the Floor	143
A Father's Anguish	145
Knit One, Purl Bloody One	147

Some of these stories are from fact while others contain a little twisting – I leave these for you to judge which is which...

The verses must be taken in the vein in which they were written...some of which are most definitely true...

Like the fox

I am an animal
Hiding
No longer human
Shying
Huddled in a corner
Underground
I'm frightened
And cold
They mustn't see
Where I am
But like the fox
My odour carries
My dirt adheres so that
When I wash
It makes me feel more
Not less
Of the creature I've become
As I crawl back
Into my hole in the ground
Vicious circle
Round and round
Can't get out
Because I'm ashamed to let them see
How low I've become

Of Soft White Nothingness

My darling remembered such a long time ago
I loved him, and love him still. In my dreams
I feel his caresses so gently around me
Surrounding me – and him
No-one can break our invisible shield
We are on an island far, far away
On a blanket of soft white nothingness
Looking down I see my body now
Time has passed leaving me helpless
Many hands – other people's hands –
Sometimes rough -touch me now
A tear drops remembering
His hands, once more, on our far
away island
Run over my face
I close my eyes remembering
Down over my shoulders
Around my shoulders
Slowly gathering me to him
I feel the warmth of his love
Filling, sweeping my very being
We are together as one – a tear falls

Cradled within his arms I am alive
The only way I can exist – but now
A tear drops on the blanket of soft white
nothingness

Bubble

Entry by invitation or interruption
Perhaps
Step outside
Into another
To make as one
Still
Intruders
Can break the seal
But the bubble is strong
Can rebuild
To cover the tear
Of intrusion

Loneliness

Loneliness
Is for
someone
else
to have
in small
doses.
Loneliness
is unbearably unbelievably sad

What a Pity

What a pity
That this city
Is full of
Sitting
Walking
Mumbling
Out of work
Homeless
People

The life of a bubble

Have you ever pondered
Over the life of a bubble
Watched as you give it birth
Your breath widening its girth
Then with wonder and open eyes
Watch it float first up then down
Bouncing in slow motion
Across the ground
Trapping your breath in its colourful film
First green and pink with youth
Changing to yellow, turquoise, brown and
purple
swirls within
Hesitates
Before the grey of age takes over
All too soon
Your breath bursts out from its captive sphere
And the bubble is no more

Fog

The fog closes
Enveloping all within
Tightening its grasp
Blinding
Confusing
Stifling
My sense of direction gone
Losing my way
Each hallowed light
Struggling
Unable to reach the ground
I feel – I feel –
Like I'm falling
Crawling
I have no eyes
Even hearing
Is strangely
Muffling
The Doppler Effect
Fear welling
Can't find my way
I can see the fog
But can't touch
Like ghostly white
That drifts away

The smell of exhausts
Lingering
Hanging
Like a gas giving death

The Green Homburg

He stood there
Proud and upright
Though
His face
All crumpled like
Dropped
Kid skin
His height and statue
Down to his black brogue shoes
Giving an air of strength
Mingled with a peculiar
Grace
The green homburg
With its neatened bow
Didn't quite go
So - I looked
Delved deeper
Without speaking
Into his face made
Of dough like rivers
Flowing, enticing you
To kneed and prod
To smooth, to see just
How deep the scars of his life could be

This Is Your Driver Speaking

"Good evening ladies and gentlemen"
in the usual cocky voice
"this is your driver speaking"
the voice slightly trying to
upgrade itself – shouldn't worry
"I must apologize for the delay"
it carries on "only there's a train
that's overshot the lights at
Gloucester Road"
Goodness I thought
just like up top in the so called
fresh air
debatable
I smile at the thought
another evening it might be
a bomb scare and
told to get on a different train
it could be
a speed restriction causing
a pile up
a Portorican reads
an office catalogue

too heavy to cart around
absorbed
girl taking up two seats
oblivious of those standing
long pink covered legs
crossed
tall Oona Chaplin type with beautiful
dark hair
long navy skirt slightly
showing beneath same coloured mac
Charles the first shoes
No buckle
her stance is straight with a kindly face
upturned nose
a figure worth remembering
"sorry about the delay but there's seems
to be
another train on the track"
wow they are having tete e tete now
I hadn't thought of that
a few minutes later and he's back
"ladies and gentlemen we should be on our way
shortly
he informs us
"I've just heard on my phone that
they have just found another driver"
wow again
firstly where did the original driver go?

perhaps to do
his shopping or
go to the loo
secondly where did they find this one?
a jumble sale or
loose wandering the streets
the mind boggles
the voice again
"yeah it's moving 'cause I can see it"
rattle of newspaper
from tired passengers
restrained amusement
the girl eventually
gives up one of her seats
we move and it becomes
just another journey

Thirty First
Anniversary Walk

Shakespearian players —much ado about
nothing
the comedy matching our spirits
a small child watching enthralled
captivated
outside the Globe on this barmy night
The Clink
a few yards further on
with cries and screams from deep within
buildings ark and ominous crowding
Ghosts of yesteryear
south past Guy's to find The George
a half galleried
three storied coaching inn
standing off Borough High Street
almost missed
no real sign no offerings of what might be
as you turn into the narrow carriageway
the cobbled courtyard
now overly tabled
where once tired steaming horses
pulled heavy coaches with their overly dressed

equally tired passengers to feed and bed for
the night
where the clatter of hooves and wheels muted
by lain straw
where strong armed full skirted knickerless
wenches would bear wooden platters
ladened with chunks of bread, cheese and
meat
along with tankards of ale
while her male customers drool over
ample flesh spilling over not so white low
bodices
cheeky gestures
easy virtue
now only tight lipped straight laced
fleshless women tucked safely
behind high bars
stating "food only in the restaurant"
everybody glumly drinking
outside
no food nor laughter
just the low hum of sedate chatter
not our cup of tea
shame
we try another pub
that's open
dead
only one 'ol boy propping up the bar

slouched
back along the Thames passed the Golden
Hind
where costumed Indian's had been making a
film
now packed and drifting away
another pub
another drinking hole with no food
thirsty
packet of crisps pint of larger
over five pounds
quiet corner easy chair to toast each other
continuing our walk the crowds have drifted
away
the makeshift theatre empty
as though it had
never been
all back in the circular building for the second
half
staff expectantly waiting
drink trolleys
behind magnificent wrought iron gates
evening drawing in garlanded
lights along the river's edge
pretty the scene through glinting jewel like
leaves
loud music from a party river bus
skateboarders pass

noise like train wheels over metal bridges
even the book stalls which we can never resist
all packed and gone
warm air wafting by the evening breeze
muted pastel banners showing us the way
we've been
fish swimming against the wind
flashes of red white and blue beyond
the dark sky heralds the coming of the night
Big Ben booms
Westminster Bridge
still tourists
though thinning mostly Japanese
wander with cameras and maps
monster cranes loom high
two men weighting with concrete
perilously close to the edge
everybody craning their necks
expectantly
we call into Lords for a sandwich
then home for a welcome cup of tea.

Without You

If you weren't here my love
I wouldn't be able to function
Without you around
I would crumble
Like burnt paper flying in the wind
Without you my life would not be the same
I remember the days when we were young
Believing you would not return
When we were apart
(I still watch from the window with
anticipation)
Together it works – we are one
I couldn't be without you
You are my staff, my rod
I need you
I Love You

The Other Side

The other side is thought of
Perhaps experienced
To one degree or another
People try not to get involved
Steer clear if told
But please don't
Come closer
To find it's not all bad
For dementia has a funny side
A beautiful side
That comes and goes
As it pleases
Not my chose – I wish it were
Then the other less pleasing side
Would not appear
The throw of the dice
Would be mine
Would disappear for all time.

Forgotten in Time

She was there
Lonely and confused
No one to hold her dear
She thought
Not her home or her things
That was precious for many a year
Now all the memories
All the love
For family and friends
Forgotten in time
She wanders
Looking, searching
For something of which
She doesn't know
Can't remember
Wandering through other people's doors
Believing them to be hers.

'You're only young twice'

I'll take my music today
We'll have a sing song
And a laugh
Remembering different times
Some bad times during the war
Rarely touched on which
I can overcome for a time
For singing and laughter
Can conquer with a
Cuddle or two
We will also take a look
At the Quentin Blake's book
I bought her
Some time ago
She thinks one drawing is of herself
Swinging from a branch
In 'You're only young twice'

Every Now And Then

She was laughing
Every now and then
Something tickled her fancy
About an old song
'A nightingale sang in Berkely Square'
Thinking the girl with the boyfriend
In the song was me
Bursting out
She was young again
For a second or two
Every now and then

Early Morning

It is six forty and I've been up for a couple of hours pottering about already. Looking out of my bedroom window it looks cold. Frost covers the ground, the shed roof is white in fact everywhere has that winter white covering – not the thick covering of snow but just enough to make you shiver. Next door must be having a shower or bath since the steam was drifting from her bathroom outlet reaching only a little way into the cold air before dissipating. The windmill sails are still against the morning mist and the slight coral sky. Morning is here and all is still quiet. In the background the low rumble of traffic along the A12 interrupts the silence now and then. I open the window to listen for bird song but can hear nothing though there is a blackbird sitting on an ariel looking extremely cold. I love the sounds of birdsong and chatter especially in the evening when the crows and pigeons are noisy, it never ceases to remind me of my childhood in Devon. The sun is rising to my left forcing orange streaks to show behind the roofs in the fast approaching daylight. The low mist is slowly disappearing though the ground frost clings on. It was a cold night last night so I put the heating on before the family stir.

I have been working on my new doll theatre, clothing the wooden structure in a pale to mid green paint. My son in law made it after seeing my pathetic attempt of woodwork and I have to admit his is far better than mine is though I will keep the original one – who knows we could have two shows going on at the same time in the future... The orange streaks seem to race across the sky now with a deeper, brighter and more dazzling colour on the horizon. I feel stimulated at the prospect of the forthcoming day.

Later I need to go shopping to buy curtain tape, hooks and rings for the theatre which is of the table top variety measuring approximately three by two by two. I managed to find some burnt orange material to make the curtains and lined them with a sort of creamy white which actually looks great with the green structure and yellow sign above. Glancing out of the window the sun is now such a brilliant red orange that without screwing your eyes up it is hard to see properly. Above this the sky has turned a pale turquoise blue, long slight clouds have an almost undiscernibly pink colour.

The dolls are all home and handmade, initially I bought a few patterns but now I make my own. The first dolls were 'elderly', eight of them. Then as the heads are made and sculpted, the more they begin to take on their own persona. It's the faces that matter on the dolls, that is when it starts to get exciting. Once they have been made then everything else follows, hair colour, style of dress, character and accessories. There are more than twenty characters and everyone different from the last.

Soon the mist will be gone and the sun will be high and it always surprises me just how fast the day turns from early morning to day once the sun decides to rise.

This afternoon I will put on a show for the elderly in a residential home which is really great fun. After the shows the dolls will be passed around to hold. Each doll has their own story which I relate which although is essentially fictional has an element of true life which the real elderly can relate to, such as the story about Cordelia. As a young girl she was a ballet dancer dancing with Rudolf Nureyev in the Bolshoi Ballet Company. Later she fell in love – with a Rag and Bone man, she hands out goldfish in plastic bags to children, and accidentally kills her husband. Then there is Cecil who was a Spitfire pilot when his best friend was shot down. Cecil was shot down too but was caught, sent to a concentration camp, he now keeps his beloved bees.

The sun is high in the blue sky now but the orangey red has gone replaced with an equally brilliant white sun. It is streaming through the gazed sliding doors and although I can't see it I'm sure the frost has gone too now.

All the same

They do it on their mobile phones - have you
noticed?
(False laugh)
That's what you hear, conversations unclear
– all the same.
Tittle tattle, wibble wabble,
all the same somehow.
Another false laugh.
On the train, in their cars, walking -
all the same.
Usually always wearing black looking all the
same.
Sort of a uniform can't think individually,
going with the flow
forgetting what makes them them. Silly fools
have they no brains,
do they leave them at home as they shower.
Like footballers really –
all the same,
the herding instinct
usually these mobile nuns
(no offence to the proper kind you
understand)
believe they've made it
aspiring to those above but

once there take pills,
have face lifts and bed one another's mate.
I suppose that is indeed their fate really.
The rest of mankind find other ways to be
the same
only the loners are left behind but they too
end up being
the same
individually.
False laugh is still there. Sometimes you get a
sort of two way thing going
where there are two of these mobile nuns
talking
but not with each other,
and have you noticed they SHOUT REALLY
LOUD.
They want you to hear.
"Oh did she?" (False laugh).
It's funny how they all develop
the false laugh isn't it.
They all do it the 'talk'
yet they don't want you to listen or understand
what they are saying.
Is it a secret code
this wibble wabble.
They could be secret agents all reporting
about those around them.

Whatever I DON'T LIKE IT SO FOR
GOODNESS SAKE SHUT UP SO WE CAN
ALL GET ON WITH OUR OWN SECRET
CODES!

Ratty

"Hey that was my stop! " isn't it always the way when you're in a hurry, get talking and miss your stop. "I told him when I want to get off too, you would have thought he would have reminded me wouldn't you. Oh blast the man now I'm going to be late. Look at him chatting up that young girl, honestly they can't think of anything else can they? I've got to get off the next one now and have a long walk. It was long enough before – and I haven't got the right shoes on for a long walk. Blast that man if only he had his mind on the job instead of that girl with her skimpy skirt nearly showing her knickers, you can almost see him undressing her, he should know better at his age. I'm going to give him a piece of my mind see if I don't." "Now look here driver I told you which stop I wanted and you've let me go right past it and all you can think of is this young lady. Hey! STOP!" Another bus stop flew by. THAT'S another LET ME OFF !" The driver glances at the young girl and winks. "Sorry love you should have rung the bell" (seeing the next stop disappearing) LOOK WHAT YOU'VE DONE NOW you silly old fool! I'm reporting you to your office!" The bus stops and the doors opened for an extremely angry woman – and now it's started to rain....soon the clip clop of her heels and muttering under her breath disappeared as the night began to draw in leaving only the constant sound of the rain and the odd vehicle passing by.

1st Poetry Meeting

We met in the Library
I was the third one there
By dribs and drabs
Hugs and kisses of long lost friends
Of knowing
Six false tea lights on table small
In a not so centred circle
Covered with a stripped satin cloth
A flask was placed within the circle
Like a ritualistic offering
Strange
Another put wine and eats on table long
With plastic glasses shinning
Book passed around
Like issues to be discussed
I didn't, initially,
See their own written words
On note pads large or small
Mine, it seemed, was the exception
My expected friend
Came late
We are the outsiders here
Everyone knows
Now silence descends
With expectation waiting for the others

That I don't know
With the fading of the sun
That had shone brightly through vast windows
Lights now on Fred, the organizer, speaks
Whispered voices except one reading Milton
Proficient in his rendering
Later learning he runs the Dylan Thomas
group
No wonder
A woman named Gillian
With a too high voice reads about
An Indian Rope Trick
Amusing
We go round one by one reading
I read 'Like The Fox'
About a man who lived in the sewers
I hope they enjoyed
Most read from books
Of published poets
Not their own
That I didn't know
Which I couldn't hear
Small voices, small sounds from most
Except the Milton man
I read
'Loneliness' and one other
When they wanted a humorous one
Called 'This is Your Driver Speaking'

Which seemed to go well
When laughter was heard
I am used to speaking at my shows for the
elderly
I like making people laugh
Also make them think of things
I find worth writing about
It probably isn't great poetry but I enjoy it
There were some excellent poets there
Much better than me
But I really did enjoy reading mine
And will go next time

April Fool's Day

The 1st of April's looming
Stay in bed
Covers over head
An appointment's booming
Feel as though I am being led
Along a path
As if fed
With milk and bread
I love the stuff
But not like this
Better with honey
Can't risk it if it's sunny
This yellow goo that's runny
Over my round tummy
Sticky gooey funny
Runny
Honey
On my tummy
Day is dawning -
Pretend I'm sleeping
Through the evening
To miss the April rising
The first almost gone now
Safe - ka pow!!!

Fat Lip at Alton Waters

(Wednesday, 06 August 2014)

Watching the sailing boats all afternoon
Lovely day
Until
Too busy I tripped
Over a mountain
Which happened my way
My footings were rocky
As stumbling downhill
The undulating ground
Opened up
To swallow me whole
I couldn't believe as in slow motion
My face sunk into the soil
With legs in the air
Arms then chest and finally
Lay sprawled on the ground
I thought how silly
Then to my rescue
Still with eyes closed I heard
"Are you alright?"

Extracting my mouth filled with grass and
earth
Slowly gathering my thoughts
And feeling my hurt mouth
"Oh I'm fine" and "It's okay I'm not bleeding"
My shinning knight, Sir Michael,
Was standing tall and shinning bright
Curly hair flowing, dressed in grey
Concern radiating throughout his frame
He leaped to my aid
Unfortunately stupid me I raised myself
Brushed myself off
"Thank you" I replied and limped away
He should have carried me off
On stallion strong to some mountain top castle
Far away
But I just felt my pride was damaged
Now the morning after
My face all swollen and aching limbs
Only think how to explain to one and all

Last Time

He lifted the horn
With loving care
For forty years they'd been a pair
Over the seas
To foreign lands
Now he played for the last time
His thoughts weren't of today
They were far, far away
How he'd chosen the horn to play
How on returning with the army band
His idol Denis Brain
Had played in Edinburgh
Driving but fatally not reaching home
His famous horn
Lay crumpled beside him

Now Terry stroking his bright and shiny friend
Remembering
Played once more part of the
Unfinished Symphony
Then quietly laid it down

Words

Words
Are like music
Flowing
Undulating
Intonation the key
Like del – fin – e – um
And fas – in – a – tion
Tonguing
Mouthing
Allowing
The sound
Of music
To come through

Incontinence Training

"Hi Miriam" it read in the text "Can you arrange to come in for incontinence training?" I didn't realize I was in need of training in that department so I dismissed it and carried on with my drawing. I was drawing one of the rag doll figures I'd made of an evacuee in the 1940's. It was coming on well and I was intending to use it on an A4 poster.

All my business cards were sitting on the table looking great. I didn't think anymore of the phone call for a couple of days until there was another. This time it wasn't the answer phone it was Helen my supervisor. I related the message adding that I didn't need it as I was fully housetrained and even have given up using Dr Whites now too!

Helen roared with laughter "Not you silly but our customers!"! As it turned out I didn't need the training anyway!.

P.S. Just a little conversation which I thought was funny, I think I ought to add that I am a home carer along with many other things.

Emphysema

My lungs are wasted
With a decease that kills
My dreams for the future
My waking hours
No longer fills
Along with my breath
My time is short
The oxygen bottle
Too frequently sought
I've fought in two wars
Been captured and caught
Put in German prison camps
Escaped – and yet
This emphysema
The last of me has set
I was never able to find a wife
Worked in the sugar beet factory
All my life
I've had some good times
And some great laughs
Made many friends
Who has remained faithful to the end
But the kind of bottle I now use
Is the kind they would want to lose
I very seldom leave my room

And occasionally it's an effort even to move
The pain is so great
So often now and
When it is too much
My whole body trembles
I cry out for God to take me
How long have I got
I'm ready now
Ready and mentally packed
But somehow I'm not sad
Only frightened of how
It will come to an end

Employers

Employers
All end up being the same
Their money
Pays your way
Demanding
Their ounce of flesh
As rapidly as they can
So
To make the job my own
I think of other things
To pass the hours along
Of poetry, green fields
My family
And home

Oh Dear She's Cooking Again

Oh dear she's cooking again
I've had to spray my room
As the smell drifts
Oh dear – I'll have to eat it
Pretend to like it – even love it
But it will be hard this time
Oh dear I've just remembered
It's probably the fish she cooked
Last weekend and kept in the fridge –
It's Thursday tomorrow!
She's going away tomorrow for a couple of
days
To Paris so her food will be great
our food will have that smell
Of decay
Of tummy upsets and feeling ill
Dare I tell her not to bother on my account
Dare I tell her I hate her food
Even though she had a cordon bleu course
I'd rather put her cooked food in the bin and
buy my own
Oh dear that awful smell

To Pick Him Up

He cries to be picked up
But I won't
Not at the moment
He's been cuddled and loved
Snuggled, fed and changed and burped
But as soon as you pop him into his cot, and
he's closed his eyes
When you think he's in the land of nod
Turn your back
There must be a switch in his head
As if on cue he opens his eyes
With chin wobbling
He cries, arms and legs flayling
If you pick him up
Tears dry up replaced by smiles

That First Smile

That first smile
First hesitant
Then as the days progress
Flashes like sun bursting
After a storm
Like the white cottages
On those magic days
When overcast grey
Is suddenly broken
With the song of a blackbird
Singing of joy

Leaving

I'm leaving you but
You're not leaving me
You'll always be there
Reminding me of what you are
I'll remember the friends who
Stuck with me through and through
When things got rather tough
After many happier times
Remember the art club every Thursday night
Held in my cottage
Where we'd paint and draw
Pot and make wonderful things
Have fun making fizzy drinks of
Many colourful hues
Suspended in space
Of the Guides, camp fires and first aid
How I loved the auctions which I'd haunt –
many items of which I bought
For next to nothing
I remember the horrors of the drunks
Of discos and broken nights
Of trying to please everybody
(which of course you can't)
Of Christmas carols and donkey and jazz
dancing in the pub car park

Of drawing from the window
Of Janet playing double bass
Of constant sweeping
Both indoors and out
Of snow and laughter
Now it will be like I've been
Passing through
Although I may keep in touch with you
If you have your ear to the ground
Once in a while
You may hear of me too

Twelve Thirty

It's now twelve thirty
Past the middle of the night
The toing and froing
Has dwindled
To the occasional
Lone person
Creeping, hurrying
To the gentle hum
Of the traffic
Sounding all muffled
A distant hum
An aeroplane
Accelerating and rising
From Stansted
Whilst another gradually falling
Too noisy
Still

Even At Night

Even at night
I love this house
Pity about the man
Two doors down
Whose wife is ill so parks his car
In our space

Even at night
This house sighs
With colourful silence
Outside
People keep coming
Past our door
Talking
Laughing
Running
Walking

Even at night

Just the way I am

So they think I'm crazy
Perhaps I am
I wonder why
I act rationally – maybe
Outspoken – well yes
I dress roughly the same
I eat roughly the same
I laugh at the same things – well sometimes
But crazy?
I am an artist, I love making things
A bit less than norm,
But crazy?
I wish I knew their definition
Then I could perhaps
Reinforce their views

What is the Matter
With You All?

What is the matter with you all
Don't you care what happens
Turn your back to the wall
See through foggy eyes
Wiping only to see
A clouded vision rise
Don't you care about yourselves
The hurt constantly given
Village mentality
Unfortunately
Is your notoriety
Don't you worry when
This very notoriety
Becomes the code
Back patting small minded power
Squashing nonconformity
Smiling throughout
Don't you think
There are people about
Who can see through
Your ineptitude
Then through their veracity
Plus your ingratitude
Leave

Such Futile Lives

Is by their thinking
I'm crazy
Really their own reflection
They can see
Through my eyes?
Is it that my outspokenness
Hurts their pride?
Or is it that they simply can't
Understand why
I'm too honest against their lies?
If so they live such
Futile, petty or unhappy lives

Headmaster

He stood there
Sweat beading and running down from temple
bright red face
trying to elongate his short statue through
stiffening back threatening posture with
shaking hands looking eyes same height as mine
as he said a defiant "no"
all I could see was anger spilling over and a
tipple or two
all too much for him
I kept my cool while he was going to pieces
all I asked was if I may take a picture of my
lovely boy when reading the scriptures in that
holy church,
he was so proud to have been asked
but the emphatic "no"
was all I received
others had taking photos but
I was being "disrespectful
in the house of God,
the vicar had said "yes" but the headmaster
thought he was 'holier' than him and knew
better.

Stream

I'm looking for a stream
A quiet minding its own business
kind of stream with stones
where the water
eddies and flows finding its way
around making patterns
as it rushes by
where stepping across is a tricky business
where leaf boats and poo sticks race against
the loud and babbling sounds
where birds dip and bathe
from hanging branches and wind rustling
leaves
where peace envelopes and all is right with the
world

Winning Through

Ending
sorry crying
leaving friends to start anew
positive thinking
is what we need
don't fear the unknown
look it square in the face
only then
just when
you're feeling blue
you will discover
that you have won through

Iris's Room

Light bright white
Pretty things upon the wall hats aplenty
beflowered and beribboned
and twenty four birds hanging
with a black and yellow song bird
in a cage

lace and corn dollies
with twiggy bird's nests
inbetween pictures of nymphs
above a wine coloured easy chair

soft music fills the air
books and mirrors galore
an open staircase to the only top floor
candle power is the name of the game
giving a glow of satisfaction
to this room of relaxation

Invisibility

"Hellooo, I am here." God how I can't stand it when they act as if I am not. As if they think I am disgusting feeding my baby.

He was hungry for goodness sake. Would you rather he screamed the place down eh?

Then there are you two (glancing at the two tramps also sitting on the bench) I'm sure you can see me, you've had ogled haven't you I've seen that look and the disgust in your eyes"

Sam looks down at her two month old son, a smile creeps over her face.

"I'm actually invisible to you all aren't I, I could do anything, you know stand on my head show my knickers – but I wouldn't do anything like that because I'm respectable – yes I am –I own my own house, my husband is working, we have a car and everything you would expect BUT –I need to feed my baby now. Actually maybe they ignore the fact that I am here but they can see those two (nodding her head in the tramps direction, they are used to seeing those around avoiding them like the plague – I do myself but I'm different , I AM JUST FEEDING MY BABY this beautiful new thing.

IT IS NOT THE SAME as those.(nodding her head towards THEM)

I know the young people can see me because one or two cover their mouths, nod in my direction and snigger but I don't mind that.

It's the adults who really get my goat. (Baby stirs and has had enough, with red chubby cheeks he sleepily turns and slightly reveals a small bit but obvious breast. Tidying herself popping the baby back in the pram she straightens up and is gone. Ignoring the two tramps.

Once more she is just a mother pushing a pram in the crowd.)

"Did you see the look she gave us —it's as though we are nothing! Just because we are down on our luck right now!"

Joe and Phil, nicknamed Carrot, "Shall we get that sandwich that woman put in there.

She only ate a couple of mouthfuls..." Joe made a slow amble to the nearest bin...

The Blue Floor

Come with me
hold my hand
the future lies before you
for this is my land

On the blue floor
I can see
the vision of propriety
even notoriety
perhaps sensuality
but never, never conformity

On the blue floor
I can see
poems galore
of times past and time to come
of colours bright – but some
to cloud over with a muted glaze
like a summers foggy haze
sad times to show with darting happiness
slowly turning the pages
of life's cages

Chubby Laughter

Ginger hair
tightly curled
blue overalls
slightly streaked with oil
newly married
creating a happy atmosphere
in pokey holes
called cockpits
screwdriver in hand
knows what he's on about
wants to be self employed
still laughing
just shrugs
and says
he can't...

Inebriation

Inebriated small minds
self opinionated
and sad
delving
into other people's lives
disrupting
too often winning –
initially

Chance Meeting

We glance
look away
glance back
as if to say
something
we brush
each others arms
as introduction
after a while talking of little things
agree to meet
soon –
can't wait
soon comes slowly
slowly
anticipation is gratified
with delight
happiness
and love

The Beekeeper

Once cottages
or hovels stood
hard lives
ghosts
now
Mr Ridgewell's
bees
making honey
almost knows them individually
rears queens
specializing
but sadly knows
the drones
enjoy
the maidens only flight

Quintet

Chandeliers
catching light
seeming to obvulate
glistening
people walking against
wind and rain
fighting
to hold umbrellas
while two people
sitting on benches
huddle together
against same rain
flights of steps
in all directions
leading to platforms
where people sit playing the killing game
consenting colours
of greys, creams and whites
with burnt sienna and red ochre
subtle changes to blur the edges of
quintet

'Soufend'

"ere we are in Soufend" remarked Maggie
"where shall we go first then?"
Flo was smelling the ozone, how she loved that
odour, all sort of clean like. It was a beautiful
day, Flo knew exactly what she wanted to do
first – the penny slot machines. She might even
see that lovely cheeky man she had met all
those years ago when she and Maggie had
come down on the coach with the whole class.
She couldn't exactly pin point the actual year
though.
He'd wanted more than what he got though.
"ere shall we dip our toes in Flo before we goes
home as well?" Maggie was talking about the
sea and Flo knew what she was thinking but
Flo's mind was racing back to her last visit to
the Kursal. Maggie was off again "do yer fink
it'll be good for me 'arfrightis Flo, yer know
paddling in the sea? Wha'yer fink?"
It had been a very hot day all those years ago
unlike today, and they were wearing pretty
summer dress – we called them sun dresses
then. Hers was a lovely blue with flowers all
over, nipped in waist and gathered skirt with
neat straps over the shoulders. She couldn't

afford a petticoat in them days so she had
pinched one of her mother's sheets to make
up. It was so heavy when she wore it but she
didn't care because when she walked and more
when they went to dances it threw her skirt
right out. She didn't care even that she
showed more of her legs than she had wanted
when she was twisted around by whoever she
danced with. Oh, those were the days.
He had sort of helped her win a big teddy at
the coconut shy then, with his help again she
had won on the penny machines too. It had
been then he stolen a kiss and wanted her to
go into the bushes with him...Although she
really had wanted to she ran to find Maggie.
Flo had kept her stupidly large teddy for years
until her children had thought it great fun to
use it in the paddling pool. Then the dog got
it... it was thrown away after that.
"do yer remember that awful big teddy yer kep
lugging around Flo, yer wouldn't let go of it
would yer even on the big wheel?"
He'd kept his eye on her for the rest of the
day even when they went to the beach but
nothing came of it, later she met her Bill. That
day she and Maggie had almost missed the
coach too.

Now Flo believes it was that petticoat that had done it and never wore it again.

When he took her hand

The night was cool
the moon high
beyond the silent breeze
through the trees a small child stood
the quiet poise of this child
belied the message on the paper
which just as silently as the breeze
drifted like a feather to the ground
the father she had know
she would never see again
never feel the hand that was so strong
when he took hers in his
now the tears flowed
as if the world had come to an end
nothing would be the same again
when the tears ceased
the world was silent
no birds sang no laughter in the air
slowly the child was no more
though she will always remember
the strength of the hand
when he took hers – then let drop so casually

Middle age

The moles on my legs
stand out against the flesh
tanned slightly around the knees
against the white duvet
brown pubic hair beneath the pale green open
dressing gown
the scared round tummy
through childbirth
and operations
punctuated by the depressed button as if to
say "that's that"
soft skin
of a natural tan
small breasts, once large and fed hungry babies
now gently rest rising and falling
with the breaths
I say to myself I wasn't left on the shelf
I'm only half done
middle age it says half way
there's still the passion
still the dreams my life has only just begun

Dreaming of Spring

The wind blowing furiously
through ill fitting window frames
chilling bones
stoking and prodding
the ovoids
knitting erratically
clacking and swearing
huddled together
in blankets and slippers
listening to the howling whilst dreaming of
spring

Well You Know
What I Mean

I've had a wonderful Christmas –
I think.
Well yes I did, you know what I mean,
Presents, good wishes and company
But towards the end, well
I didn't want to feel blue
I wanted it all to go out with a bang
Sort of,
You know see the New Year in
But as I said towards the end
It sort of fizzled to a stop.
It was the car, it started to make this noise
You know what I mean,
A grinding noise that's what it was
That passers by turn to see what the racket
was
That made you want to keep your eyes
Straight ahead, avoiding theirs,
Know what I mean?
Well it got worse, this noise,
To a fierce grizzly groan
As though its throat was sore

Well to cut a long gruesome story short
The garage wants eight hundred pounds to put
it right
Well I did say you know what I mean
And I was right.

Perfect Job

I had the perfect job
For me that is
Everything was right
As I put in my all
Then when I arrived
One Wednesday morn
Told it wasn't there after all
Redundant, gone
It really isn't fair

Physiotherapy

Mr Potter is tall dark and amazingly handsome. Need I say more. Oh and a lovely sense of humour. His face lights up when he smiles with a twinkle in his eye that does not invade my 70 year old sexual passion just alights my own sense of liking. I have been to other physiotherapists, chiropractic's and acupuncturists but have failed to keep it up as they didn't do anything for me other than cause more pain but I will see if I want to come back here after a day or two.

It all started when I had a head on car accident on the 9th of January 2010. I ended up with a cracked rib, the dashboard hitting my knees leaving damage mostly on my left knee, bad bruising across my chest and a car that was a write off. My head had bounced back and forth three times too. At the time I burst into tears because I now didn't have my little car and with my husband's car also off the road he would have to go to work on his bike whereas I couldn't get to work at all plus we didn't have the money to get another car.

Luckily I had a camera in the car and although I was injured I had the foresight to take photographs of the damage to both cars along with the tyre marks etc which came in very useful when claiming against the other side.

In the other car were three young foreign boys who I believe thought they were driving in their own country of origin so on the wrong side of the road. We decided to go to the bank to get a loan in order to get another car, and found another Ford Fiesta but three years older and more basic however it did allow me to go to work. We had to get Terry's car sorted out which cost us a further £300 as it was still winter with it's dark nights and he had come off twice whilst riding along the A12 which doesn't have street lights. The cycle lane dips down in a particularly dangerous place where car lights don't reach also the tarmac crumbled away towards the drainage ditch which ran along the edge of farmland. This was where he wobbled, put his foot down to steady himself falling roughly six feet into the ditch and tangled in brambles. Brambles had overgrown along with tree roots and general vegetation. If he had knocked his head nobody would have found him. His bike had landed on top of him. Meanwhile I was getting worried since he had not come home at the usual time, when he did open the door he face was scratched as were his hands and legs. Only a week later he fell at exactly the same place so we decided we had to something and get his car back on the road.

When I visited the Doctor I asked for a sick note to pass onto my office he quite angrily stated that "he can't for a crashed car"....eventually giving me a week off. I wouldn't mind but as a home carer there was no way I could do what would be expected of me. A week later I went back, he gave me a further week. I should have laid it on thick but I am rather too truthful for my own good sometimes. However although I wasn't really ready I restarted my work just three weeks after the accident. It was about six months after this that I applied for the 'no win no fee' insurance against the young foreign man who ruined my car, forced me to buy another car, damaged me, my husband falling off his bike times two and forced us to get his car mended which we were going to scrap. This has entailed me filling out numerous forms, a visit from a man from the solicitor, a visit to a bone man in Colchester and recently an assessment by the delicious Mr Potter. I now have to wait for his bill to send to the solicitor, asking for them to ring him for the written assessment and how many sessions I will need. At the moment he is stating 6 – 8 so I wait with abated breath.

I still am not sure if I'll go back though.

The Rebirth of Mankind

From the sphere of the sunflower
The petals are shed
One by one
Generously
The bubbles float
Above the ground
Giving birth to mankind
Wandering aimlessly
But I
I have escaped
I see, watch and observe
Recording their feeling
Their meanderings
Their unhappinesses

Flu

Here I am
Writing
Not sleeping
As I ought
Oh I have tried
Actually got off to the land of nod
Three times
But
Three times
Coughing and sneezing
So I thought I might as well sit it out
Do something useful instead

Nits and Lice

It was three o'clock am when I found the little buggers. I had been scratching my head for a number of weeks but thought it was an allergy not the real culprits of which I had no knowledge. Just the thought of them while I am writing this gives me the creeps. I had spread a black plastic sheet over my lap and thoroughly brushed and combed my hair to see if I had dandruff or something. I was horrified to see things moving, actually moving on the sheet. I rushed to find the magnifying glass and peered through it. I couldn't believe that I must have been carrying these creatures around. My grandson, had been scratching also before I had started so he must have them too. I felt dirty and couldn't understand why I hadn't realised before. I had never had them before nor had my children when they were young. Immediately I wanted a shower and to scrub my scalp clean. Upstairs I ran the water and removed my pyjamas, stepping underneath the water, wetting my hair I poured the medicated shampoo all over. For ten minutes I scrubbed and scratched using more shampoo than I needed. It was still very early so tried not to wake the other members of the household. However I didn't feel I could put my pyjamas back on so I went into the bedroom and sitting on the edge of the bed I told my husband about the find, there was no way I could get back into bed until the sheets were washed. I so needed a cup of tea. My husband came down all bleary eyed. We sat drinking and discussing the situation. There was nothing we could do until the shops open and it was a Sunday and won't open until ten o'clock and I had to go to work as a carer knowing I had creepy crawlies running about on my head – ugh! I can't tell my customers because they would have a fit if they knew. My mother grew up in a street in London next door to the local nurse who held a nit clinic every Saturday morning and seeing children queue up waiting to go in to be deloused, so she would have been horrified to learn we had nits and lice in this day and age, thankfully she is not with us anymore so she won't know. I read up on the internet about the creatures which told us that they are only passed on from close contact from head to head, they can't jump, hop or fly but they hide when you scratch or brush your hair. Washing does not wash them out since the little buggers cling on

the hair using their hooked feet! The only way
to get rid of them is special lotion and a nit
comb. Can't wait!!. I tried every 'remedy in the
chemist but in the end the only thing that got
rid of them was combing with a nit comb over
the sink as often as I could each day! It took a
few days but oh what a relief – I can't tell you
the satisfaction with no more itchy scalp...that
was a couple of years ago now and would
advise anyone, especially when there is a
outbreak of the horrible things at school to do
the same..no need to spend on anything other
than a comb.

The Dell

The ropes swung high
Above the dell
Looking back I can't believe
I could have climbed up – let alone getting
down again
To and from our tree houses – our club houses –
Held tightly within the branches
Of thickly trunked giants surrounding
The rim of a bomb hole.
I remember looking down to the dizzy depth
Of the bottom of the dell
Girls squealed as the two swings squeaked
Backwards and forwards
Mottled sunlight played on the soft grass
Mowed frequently
And the stingers which grew abundantly
The steep slidey slopes
With homemade bows and arrows
Carefully cut and strung
We'd fight out our wars
Defending our camps
From the opposing side
While squawking geese defended theirs.

Far Distant Valleys

Seclusion is the room for one
Imagination is the room for one
To allow my thoughts a free reign
To climb the heights
Between time and space

In this room of peace and tranquillity
I close my eyes
Sitting quietly
Within my mind are
Gentle movements
Dreamy movements
Of far distant valleys
With a secret door
That could lead to
Anywhere.

No Right

What is she playing at
Mum I mean
She thinks I haven't the right
She thinks
I haven't the know how to find our past
To find our Dad
She thinks
She knows so that's that
None of our business
So I'm told
Spitting the words venomously
Hating the very idea of possible discovery.
Years now – on the brink
Fearing too late
Hard to find a relative
To speak
His or her mind
Yet
The age of discovery is not dead
Anticipation thrills
Participation Kills
Those spiteful eyes

The years of searching
May be ending soon
Meanwhile
Excitement still.

Matron Greenslade

Matron Greenslade how horrid you were
With your straight hard face
Inclement eyes
Pearl necklace, dark suit
And horn rimmed glasses
Suited your short cropped hair
And determined chin
Sitting in your sumptuous study
With Chinese rugs and squashy sofa
Sending orders
Venturing out only for discipline,
Prayers and medication
Such as bitter aloes and syrup of figs
The only friendship that you upheld
For Miss Johns, her baby
And the Siamese cats
For us, the girls your spiteful tongue and
beating hand
Was all we saw.

Childhood Beckons

A smell or maybe a touch
Instantly you are back
Amongst the fairy heads
As your childhood beckons

With me it's the smell of polish,
Of sewing, dancing, carbolic soap,
Syrup of figs and midnight feasts

It's hard to imagine
Back in the days of yore
That the other girls memories
Are so different to mine
For I remember the fun we had
Of creativity and sharing,
Of shows, dressing up boxes,
Of dodging the sharp eyes of the staff,
Of being caught and given
Endless lines and heavy chores
To think of my childhood days
It's not despondency and gloom
But something to carry me my whole life
through

The Chestnut Tree

My hand involuntarily went to my mouth
As a gasp left my mouth
She stood there
Happily
As yet another branch fell
Thinking only of future shaded sunlight
Now gone
The man with dirty face and crazy eyes
Swung deftly in mid air
Held from thick ropes tied
The saw humming to cover
The cries from the mutilated tree
"Look Mummy" said the two year old
"Be careful" and "Don't fall"
Higher and higher went his saw
Higher than the council allowed
She clapped her hands
"How wonderful to see"
The majestic chestnut tree cried out in vain
But only I could hear
The roaring fire threw up it's smoke
Swirling blotting out the view
Our squirrels, jays and jenny wren
Would they come back again?
All but the top most branches

Like some ludicrous hairdo
Remained
Fifty feet above the ground below this
'crowning glory'
Untreated scars
As big as dinner plates allowing the rot to set
in
My complaints go unheeded
I am treated with disdain
Triumphantly she thanks him
Tipping his open hand
It's dark now
Apart from the flames
Showing her nakedness,
Humiliation and shame.

Silken Threads

The silken threads
Of childhood
Holds
Like nothing else can
Pulling you back to the innocent days
Of youth
When fears and worries
Were confined
To the golden box
Protected
By time

Half Forgotten
Dreams

I'd almost forgotten those dreams of long ago
When we would sit
Amongst the fairy heads
Of dandelions
While eating their vinegar tasting leaves
And pulling off the legs
From grasshoppers
Then finding them homes
With woodlice in holes in trees
Do you remember
Believing we could and would
Fly down the stairs
And down the lane
I can feel it now
How I used to feel
I've never changed
Have you?

The 'pulling off legs from grasshoppers' refers
to try to stop my father running off when I
was three and a half. If he didn't have legs he
wouldn't leave.

Romania

I was lost
Couldn't find my way
Stopped an old couple
Although the language
Only a few words I could say
Eventually
Led to a building
Behind green railings
Then upstairs
To a small office with bars
Thought about
Not being allowed to get out
Fear momentarily
A little man with grey curly hair
Elfish, bright eyes smiling
Picked up the phone
Proceeded to call
About fifty people in all
To find an interpreter then left the room
For ten minutes or more
On returning carrying paper small
Carefully
I puzzled stood up looking into his eyes

As he presents me with
Two walnuts – shelled
I was overwhelmed
I didn't know what to do
For I instinctively knew
He'd given me his all

Alone

Alone
By yourself not
With another
To call your name
Alone
With your own thoughts
Flying
Inside your head
Loudly
Alone
Miserably
Trying
To keep sane

Will People Care

I draw and do my art
To live
To share
But will people care
Will I be allowed
For they want you to fail
By winning
You seem to threaten their existence
That's what separates
You and me
I to give, you to take
I to show how low
How low we are all to oblivion

Travelling Companions

The couple got on at Tottenham Hale
Both were thin though
She was shorter than him
As they stored their large tapestry bag
She glanced my way
Making me shudder
Her witch like eyes
The colour of a winter sky and pallid skin, as
his,
Matched the way she viewed
Her travelling companions
Blocking the gangway
The guard asked them to move to the next car
Ushering firmly through the carriage
Muttering they passed
I had a feeling they would be back
To claim the unpaid for first class seats
After the guard disappeared
And I was right

For Art's Sake

Art for art's sake
Is not my answer to the stakes
For I feel a lust for paint
For creativity the day is wasted if I don't
create
My way to illusion so deep inside my frame
When confronted with the beauties
And the wrongs
Of this our society

Post Natal Depression

Rant and rave
Kick about
Throw the baby to the ground
It's not me that's not got
My feet upon the ground
I want to shout
I want to cry
Sleep the whole day through
But all I seem to be able to do
Is be a slut and shut
The world and people out
Please let me be myself again
I love my baby
Want to kiss and cuddle
But all I hear
All I hear are
Screams
And wet nappies hanging about
So
Before I can say
I love you
I've thrown the baby

Yet again
To the ground

This was written after I had seen a young girl
on the television in court who had killed her
baby. I imagined what it would be like to be
her . I hasten to add I have not been in that
position ever.

A Witch's Spell For Winter

Crunchy white
Spraying high
Light of sky
No dark light
Nipping fingers
Toes as well Not forgetting tip of nose
Children laughing
Can't control
Slipping and sliding
Tears as well
Salted roads
Too infrequent
Tyres and metal
Bumping, crunching
Stay indoors the old to tell
Frightened even to answer the bell
Waiting for the sun
Forgetting the fun
Had when young
Dogs running madly
Enjoying but badly
Soiling the white, white snow

The Commode

I sit on the commode
I wait
I sit on the commode
I wait
Time passes
My mind wanders
I dream
Of other things
I sleep
"Have you done yet?"
I jolt
My mind wanders again
"Come on let's see"
I am lifted
"No now come on – try!"
I try
My mind is wandering again
Mindless I dose
"...well never mind
Try again another time"
I am lifted
Finished.

Maggie

Maggie
I cried when I saw you on the telly
Oh Maggie I cried
I wanted to envelope you
Fold my arms around you
Especially
As you opened your life for all to see
Then you cried
You could so easily have been
Anyone of us
In these recession blues
So I whisper
There but for the grace of God
Go I

The Rape

He was –
God how do you describe
This sort of animal
Words are too good
To use on this abysmal
Falsehood
Humiliation
Was his theme
Defiling
Her body on the ground
Nothing can replace
What he took
At his own pace
Again and again
She lost all
What did he lose?

The Abandoned Babies

Their eyes were loud with silence
Watching
Their tiny hands clutching
Entwining
Left with right
Tightly
Tiny infested bodies
Lying sinking
Stinking
Into sodden mattresses
Encased in prison like bars
Captive dirty and rusting

The year is now
The time is crying
Dying
For love

Tuesday, 01 April 2014
Cardiac Failure and fluid in the lungs

Well what a shock when I went back to see the doctor. Last week I had an appointment because I thought I had asthma. I saw a lovely young doctor called Dr Townsley who sent me downstairs to have an ECG, blood pressure taken and pulse rate done by the nurse. I was told to wait because the doctor wanted to see me again. Back in her surgery Dr Townsley told me it looks as though I have had a heart attack at some point though not in the last few weeks. She asked me to go for an Xray at the hospital soon. I went the same day – better sooner than later. The next morning I was called to make another a appointment because the doctor would like to see me again...the earliest was the following Monday which was yesterday.

I was seen by my usual doctor, Dr Verrill. He told me of the Cardiac Failure and asked me what I thought that meant..I replied 'Yes that means I'm dying!' 'No' he told me 'It's curable now, about twenty years ago it wasn't but things have moved on since then'...Apparently the left side of my heart has all but stopped...the pump and the electrical impulses have stopped working and I have fluid in the lungs...I asked why but he doesn't know so I had to have more tests like to see if my kidneys, liver, calcium, celestial etc were at the right level trough blood test and I am to have a echo sounding of my heart. Downstairs again I had the blood tests but have to wait for the appointment for the echo sounding as someone has to come from the hospital so have to wait for an appointment. Thankfully he/she will go to the surgery so I won't have to go to the hospital. Dr Verrill gave me some pills to tide me over until the blood tests come through and I've another appointment for next Monday. Unfortunately the hospital test won't be through by then so that will be a further appointment I suppose unless I can be seen by the doctor on the same day.

Dr Verrill is very curious as to why this is happening to me so hence the investigation. However lets go +back to when I broke my rib last December the 8th after which I developed a cough which wouldn't go. At the time Dr

Verrill sounded my chest telling me I had fluid in my right lung. He gave me antibiotics for one week. These didn't have the desired effect because the cough continued. I still have it and it is now April. But let's go back even further to when I went in for a blood test at the end of July last July. The results of which were that I had high cloistral and advised to exercise. I started to walk down to the town and back a distance of about two and a half miles. Going down was okay but coming home is uphill and as I walk generally at a fast pace by the time I got home I had a pain in my chest and found it difficult to breath. I took it I was very unfit but made every excuse not to do it too often. Terry kept onto me at every opportunity so much so that it became a broken record. Anyway now I think it was probably the start of what is wrong now -o in fact it probably has been going on for a lot longer however I used to walk well so something happened at some point.

When I was a girl in Dr Barnardos Homes the doctor came every week. I know I fainted frequently so I assumed that was the reason I was seen each time. Each time I was asked to walk a straight line, he sounded my chest and asked the member of staff a few questions then I left the room. I never was told why I was summoned each time – sometimes the only girl who went in. As I grew up I still had fainting spells even when I married. One time when I was working for the Brains I told Sue Brain in the morning I couldn't work that day because I was feeling faint. She told me to go back to bed and called the doctor. When he arrived he actually gave me an internal! At the time I didn't realized that that was what it was but an internal it was. Blooming cheek! Anyway I continued with the fainting spells in fact only very recently I had one though not a full passing out one. I have always had periods where my blood sugar was low but the answer to that was always to have something to eat quickly.

Anyway I am now taking the pills Dr Verrill gave me last Monday and they do seem to be working – perhaps a little too well since I have slowed down quite dramatically which maybe a good thing since everyone kept telling me I was doing too much with the theatre, June, Mollie and for a short time Brigget too.

End of day three with not a lot to report really only that apart from coughing a lot wearing myself out, sleeping for one and a half hours this morning and again during the afternoon I feel I am rather better than on Monday so the pills are working. I can however still feel the rattle in my chest though. Oh and I have lost weight too which can't be bad. The pollution outside has been bad but since I am not going out it doesn't affect me. Both Iris and Penny called me about it but assured them both I would not be going out during this week. Had call from Liz too but offering help should I need it. I probably will do next week but waiting for my next appointment with Verrill to find out what has been discovered.

Last night I didn't sleep well. Although I went to bed at my usual time of nine and fell asleep, I woke two and a half hours later...came downstairs and had a cuppa, read for a while, upstairs again and slept until around four thirty with a tummy ache so went to the loo. I won't say too much about that only that I was constipated. I left the bathroom feeling exhausted. Couldn't get to sleep again because I shouldn't have tried so hard as my chest was hurting...Anyway it is now the fourth day. I tried some ironing but I started to feel too hot and not quite right so only got one top done. The phone rings twice, the first time it was Iris, my sister saying that if I need her give her a call. The second was Liz virtually saying the same however this week I am doing very little and next will be school holidays with Monday taken up with another awaited visit to Verrill which can't come soon enough.

Wednesday, 16 April 2014

A couple of weeks have gone now and I must admit I do feel a bit better. I am sleeping without the attacks which allow me to lay on my back as well as my usual right side. However I am still waking up after only two or three hours. Even my wind has reduced. I do get tired easily though I haven't got the pain in my chest. I know I still have the fluid in my lungs though not as bad because I can feel it when I breathe deeply rattling around. I have restarted my shows but am not going to do the homes that I consider to be badly run or that have bad vibes because they just cause stress which I can do without. I have an appointment for a further blood test which is for the kidney and the echo sounding of my heart. However I couldn't get another appointment with Dr Verrill since he is off sick and isn't expected to be back soon. He did say he wanted to see me in four weeks but I reckon he knew he'd be going back into hospital till then. Anyway I have provisionally made an appointment with Dr Townsley and hope Dr Verrill will be back to see me on the fourth week visit. I do hope so. If he is I shall transfer my appointment to him on the 6th of May. He is only working on one kidney and that's very poorly. He may have to retire early and once again I do hope not. Oh and I have started swimming exercises in Deben Pool, since you are suppose to tell the instructor if you have any medical problems I did, however all she said was "Anybody can come!" repeated at least three times!! So now I'm an 'Anybody!' Not the right response I would have thought. Does she have any medical training?!! I fear not. It's a good job that I know the tell tale signs of an attack now and can monitor myself! One of the women who also was swimming was surprised too when I told her! I think the instructor didn't believe me – well I do look well I suppose. All the women were taking bottles of water or orange (gin and orange?) so maybe I ought to take some (water) as well though it is only for an hour and feel it isn't really necessary. Some women also had little socks with those slip proof spots on the soles. They told me it stops their feet from sliding on the bottom of the pool. So perhaps I should get a pair as well.

7.7.14

Had an appointment with Dr Verrill this morning to see if I still need a pill which wasn't on my list. He couldn't understand why there was no mention of the furosimide in my records which he remembers giving along with the other six pills. No sign of it. I didn't say but Dr Weeks sounded my chest and told me there was 'no fluid in my lungs' so I think it he who took it off my list however if it was he had no reason to interfere with my historical records! I asked Verrill if my childhood 'fits' and my dizzy spells on waking had anything to do with my current problem. The 'fits' no but really couldn't say because he wasn't my doctor then. The dizzy spells he didn't think so because they have been happening for such a long time. He took my blood pressure which was normal and sounded my chest which wasn't. I still needed the flurosimide due to fluid! I remarked that I didn't expect to have anything done at the hospital appointment tomorrow and Verrill agreed except possibly increase a couple of pills which he will be doing anyway. I asked if I would ever come off the medication to which he said THAT HE WAS HOPING TO AT SOME STAGE. So now we wait until tomorrow when I see Doc

Venables at 12. Apparently I have another at 12.30 too so....

The appointment yesterday was quite short though I was seen quite quickly. I had another ECG then was taken to wait to see Dr Venables. After a few questions he sounded my heart, took my pulse and blood pressure then said he would like to show me something...it was the echocardiograph. I could see the image of my heart which he explained the large black patch was the area where if the valves worked properly would close with the rhythm of the heart. However mind was quite literally just a flutter rather than a closure. He explained that it was a very serious condition and just a few years ago would have been a death sentence with no reprieve...however now a pacemaker would regulate the signals giving me a much better chance and my life back. He was writing to Dr Verrill to up my medication and I would have a letter giving me another appointment within six weeks to have an angiogram and tests to check if my valves are strong enough for a pacemaker to be fitted. He repeated it was a very serious condition. It makes me wonder first of all why had an appointment I initially had last month been cancelled and why had it

taken four months for me to see Dr Venables since it was considered to be an 'urgent' request for an appointment? I can understand why the first time cardiac failure was mentioned in my records in 1981 why I wasn't told and why I hadn't even seen the specialist...it has only been a few years since pacemakers were able to be fitted and give the recipient a better life span. In my records it keeps mentioning 'patient does not need to know'...I will ask Verrill but I really know the answer which is staring me in my face. I sent a message to Penny to have herself and boys checked since it can be hereditary, she called me back pretty quickly so we could have a chat. Jamie didn't seem concerned at all only that it was Gabbie's birthday tomorrow! When Nic was due to go into have her gall bladder removed dur to gall stones you would have thought she was dying but my life is not of concern!!!Deary me. I know I make light of it but I would like a little concern from his part especially now. Even when I said it might be good to be on the safe side to get his and the girl's heart checked all he said was that he had had his checked and it was alright.
Thursday, 18 September 2014

Had a call this morning from the hospital, I have an appointment for the angiography next Thus the 25th of September. That'll be almost 7 months since the referra which was supposed to be 'Urgent'l! Well at least it is moving forward now...
To be continued....

The Circumcision

I've just witnessed
The circumcision
Of a ten month old boy
He screamed on cue
(Apparently the right thing to do
For screaming releases adrenalin
So that shock can't set in)
Believe that if you will!
The doctor, after instructing
A male friend on how to hold
The wriggling infant,
Naked on a cushion of towels
Placed on the front room coffee table
In the speckled sunlight
Shinning through the heavily laced
Bay window
Started pulling back the foreskin,
Tearing the foreskin
To expose the tiny head
Then with an instrument that looked
Like a stubby tuning fork
With a tight pencil thin slit
Three quarters it's length
Pulled the loosened skin
Through, still pulling the baby screams

Louder, with the fork in place
Head protected
And limbs held
Froglike with equal force
His face so white, small and trembling
The doctor's blade glinting
In the summer sun
Snipped off the so called unwanted flesh
Still the baby screaming
The sutras one, two and three
Around the bloody shaft
Bandaged he is given to me
waddled, exhausted
He falls asleep
Passed to his mother next door
After a cup of tea
She rocks him
Apologetically
Therapeutically
Neither of his parents slept last night
Nor in fact had I knowing
That the deed
Was not for religion or health reasons
Just to be like him
Now with a sigh of relief
The doctor draws a diagram with shaking hand
For them to see.
I wondered if the parents had seen the act

Or even performed the deed
Would they, I wonder,
Have had second thoughts
Then just cradled baby small instead.
Now the morning after
After a night of torment and dread
I remove the dressing
To expose the naked head
Reflecting what was left
I tell myself
To circumcise a girl
Must be far worse
To mutilate, disfigure and maim
In body and mind
If I understand it correctly
The only reason to circumcise a girl
Is so that she would feel no pleasure
No wanderings to other men
To trap her to one – her husband
How can these parents live with themselves
Would they, I wonder,
Mutilate themselves
Disfigure
So that when on the wedding night
Have to be cut to allow natural relations to
happen lovingly
Or when the young girls go into labour can't
enjoy the act

They usually have several children so would
have to be cut each time and
Each time would have to be a bigger cut
Because the old scar would be taken out
The poor girls
I'm so glad I was not them.

You Never Know

School teacher is on the train again
No book only paper
Turned to the sport
A pigeon flies in at Earls Court
Then out through the
Next door as if to recognize its
The wrong journey
Grey day – overcast
Street lights glowing
Weakly
Nobody gets on at Barons Court
The train waits expectantly
The lights shine
In the Ark
Beneath a high crane
Here an Inca conquering Spaniard
And a Samurai
The other day a Pre Raphaelite
Or two with Rossetti hair
You never know just who you'll meet
From one journey to the next
Gangsters also compete
With molls dressed in their own fashion
With cockney voices and rings galore
Furs and gold for sure

Passing drugs look my way
I shrink into my seat
You never know just who you'll meet

They Took Him

They took him he was gone, gone
I went with him found it hard
To leave, leave him there
Alone with others who didn't love him
One day he'll be back
One day I would so love
To be today, tomorrow
But fear it will never come
Now he comes for weekends
Every other to love and cherish
But they say he has to forget
The things of yesterday
The things he enjoyed, he loved
The things which brings remembering
If he doesn't come home for good
He will be another
Whom we don't know
Or him us
They told us we needed therapy
They told us we were angry
No arguments if we want him back
We have to be better than
Good enough parents if we want him back
But we don't offer a threat
Only commitment, protection
And love of the proper kind

It's Pam Again Tomorrow

It's Pam again tomorrow
To carry on from last week
For her to tell me
That anger = annoyance and the like
I have to convince her of my agreement
And understanding to move on, to stand back
Which is hard but it has to be done
Since I don't believe anything
That comes out of her mouth
But it has to be done
Whatever I have in my mind
In order to get my grandchild back

The Wait

Empty streets
Save for the odd car
Now and then
Sun rays racing from right to left
Giving long shadows
From trees and houses
Across the road
Peaceful
An empty seat put there by someone long gone
The paper boy moving onto another street
On this bright morn all quiet and still
With buds waiting to burst Early this year
That's another job done
Now waiting for the next
For the right time
Too early until nine am
Just want to get done
Only two more
Then home

Old Bill

He's nearly one hundred
Believes the photograph of his son's
Wedding is him
Mentally he's pretty good – more or less
He just sits there
Tearing tissues into small pieces
In a weird way
To make them last longer
Something within him feels the need
To tear, tear and more tearing
To wipe the weepy eye
With as small a piece as possible
The one which has drops in
Three times per day
He worked on the land
By all accounts quite a lad
In his day
He cries, can't see through almost blind eyes
When tears flow

Still the music plays on

There's a film on the tele
Filled with violence
To a high degree
But the music is terrific
Makes you want to weep
Contrasting greatly
My boys watch avidly
Cheer when see the boxer go down
Even more when blood spurt
Then won't leave the room
Eyes glued to the room
I hate to see
I churn within
Can't look
Typ faster
To block out the din
But then
Just when
I get stuck in
They turn the dam thing up
A cheer goes round
Someone is down

I look up
I really feel sick
For on the tele
Someone's on his belly
Being kicked and punched
And more
Then the music comes back
To fill the gap
Between yet more violence
Oh why do the insist
On showing these scenes –
Still the music plays on –
The boxer, with a roar from the crowd
Makes his way to the ring –
The music, beautiful music –
The referee calling
Death lurks
Round nine then ten
Violence just below the surface
The whole film through
Do they have to fight and sprawl?
Can't we just love one another
And listen to the music in peace

The Primitives
to the End

From time to time violence has always
Reared it's ugly head throughout the age of
man
The need to survive has oft' been the cause –
Or the excuse –
But I wonder, is there really more
Or is it just so well documented within the
media?

There used to be – burning at the stake
For suspicion or a whim
Branding, tongues cut out
And the wearing of the chastity belt
Scold's bridles were the rage
Which really put the wife in a cage
With the ducking stool
To see if the truth you did or didn't tell
Or your dues you couldn't pay
The stocks awaited you
To delight the passer by
With a rotten egg or two

Perhaps as a child you were sent to work
Whipped an mistreated
Or sold to slavery
If you managed to survive all of these
You most likely were the victim of a robbery
Today we have not quite all of these
In this our lives a new one has become rife
This one is one of drugs
Many die in misery
Because it captures their lives totally

Since someone invented fire
And one man has had the edge
Another has always wanted to
Push him off the ledge
Again and again and again
Though some show considerable concern
Will man never learn?
It seems as though we are destined to remain
The primitives to the end.

My Son's In Trouble

I've a friend at last
Said my son one day
Great said I
Where does he live and what's his name?
The friendship grew
(Or so I thought)
For my son the time flew
He came round, this friend so called
But more often than not they went out
Then came the day
When I was called on the telephone
My son's in trouble
Along with his friend
Been put in a cell
For an hour or two
He's frightened and scared
What can I do
What can I do
He has burgled
To keep his friendship
To him so true
Oh why didn't I see it
Why couldn't I listen to my inner self
When I felt
Things weren't going

The way I thought they ought
Now a solicitor sought
It is c
Going to court
Too late his lesson taught.

The Cigarette

Walking with a friend one dark night
We were beset upon by three
One had a knife
Another a bayonet
Whilst the third a cigarette
'Where are you going' said number three
Allowing my friend to go through
My back against the wall
The knife was thrust against my chest
The bayonet to my neck
Then number three with his cigarette
Burnt my face not once but thrice
The pain was fierce
I didn't move I didn't writhe
But cried inwardly
Then once more the cigarette stubbed on my face
This time it went out
'Now you've put my fag out'
He laughed and walked away
With his friends one and two
Number one got off when came to court
Numbers two and three are on probation
I hope their lesson taught
My face has now healed
But in my memory it remains.

Across the Floor

There was a girl
Who didn't want to unfurl
The love she had
Inside that body so sad
Shunned from touch
Which was almost too much
For this girl to cope with

This girl now growing older
Still unable to show her love
Almost in fact got colder
Her parents wanted desperately to show
Their love but find it difficult to know how

There is no respect
There is no sign
That there will be a future
For the love that tries to fill
The valleys and the hills
Of this life of hers

The parents wish for her to take their hands
To share the land
Of her imagination
Like she used to do

But this girl
With so much to offer
Who is so much softer
Than she appears to be
Cannot open the door
Go across the floor
To what lies beyond.

A Father's Anguish

He sits there quietly
The smoke from his pipe
Curled
Through the open window
The rustle of newspaper
The only sign
Of inward unhappiness
Exaggerated only a little
Of this otherwise calm exterior

His daughter walks through
Doesn't see
Doesn't want to see
Doesn't want to feel
Or give
To this man who is her father

Why is she doing it?
She doesn't even know
Of that I'm sure but still
It can't hide
What is inside
For father and daughter
Don't know how to resolve
The anguish felt and hurt constantly given
By daughter to father

No one sees his cry
No one hears him scream
For he hides
Beneath
The smoke curling
Above the window pane
And behind the news of
Other people's pain.

(Here are two cockney ladies with hearts of gold. Maggie is fuming after an argument with her husband and when that happens 'lets off steam' as it were. Please forgive the single repeated swear word she uses to vent her feelings. She really does have a heart of gold as when the story unfolds you too will realize it. However I don't excuse their cockney language as it really is the way they speak.)

Knit One, Purl Bloody One

"Knit one, purl bloody one, don't know why I chose this stupid colour anyway. 'e don't even like grey. Nondescript that's wha' I call it; mind yer grey's great on some people – not 'im though – maybe that's why I chose it, sor' of a parting gift you might say, somefin to remember me by. Oh 'e'll throw it no doubt but wha' do I care I'll be out of 'is 'air before 'e knows what's happened....."

Maggie was talking to Flo her best friend since early school years. Their Mum's were best friends too long before the girls got together. Flo was used to Maggie going on and hardly ever interrupted her 'flo' as it were. If it wasn't grumbling about her Fred then it was something else.

"....an' do yer know what 'ees 'as gone an' done now?" not waiting for an answer "'ee's bloody gone an' took me 'oliday money wha' I've bin saving fer ages, tha's what 'ees gone an' done, that's all!" adding "ere pass us one of them marzipan tea cakes Flo love" Flo had been so pleased with herself when she had found the old sweets in a tuck shop that she had never been to before. She had wandered down an unfamiliar side street. Rows of the old sweet jars had lined the shelves selling all the old fashioned goodies. Flo had been transported back to childhood and the joy of choosing a couple of ounces of the delicious sweets was sheer delight.

Maggie was working herself up good and proper that's for sure thought Flo, into a right 'ol state if you ask me but time had shown Flo that Maggie soon cools down if you just let her rant on. They were going by train to Exeter to see a long lost school friend they had just heard from. It was all a mystery where Daphne had been all this time but soon they will find out as she has promised to 'tell all' when they see her. "Ees well off ain't ee" Maggie points to the man asleep in the corner with her knitting needle "I wish ee'd close 'is mouth an' stop snoring!" Everybody in the carriage turned to look at the sleeping man especially when a loud SNORE escaped. There were several smiles and sniggers.

Maggie had finished the ribbing and was onto the main body, knit one row then purl the next. She liked knitting, her mother had taught her as a young child and it usually calmed her down but this time was different. The sway of the train was doing it's trick for her instead. Towns came and went with the changing into countryside and weather so soon her mood had changed too. "Scuse me Mam but could yer ask yer nipper to stop opening the winda when we goes through the tunnels 'cause all them smuts is gettin' in me eyes an' on me knitting too" The boy is pulled to the mother "thanks Mam so kind" Maggie turns back to her friend....

"Do yer remember Flo when we was girls 'an we was on tha' coach?" her thoughts had turned to their childhood "where was it we went Flo?"

again not waiting for an answer "oh I remember now, it was to Soufend weren' it. Do yer remember? Oo we had some fun then with 'ol Mr Flanagan didn't we" this wasn't a question "when we pretended we was lost down in that Kursall place." She had reached the arm pits and was decreasing six stitches as if by memory, she was so lost in her thoughts she was hardly looking at her knitting "ee was in a right 'ol tiswas weren' 'e, we could see 'im but sure as eggs was eggs 'ee couldn't see us though. Do yer remember we was almost weeing ourselves."

"Tickets please" the ticket collector called as he opened the door to their carriage "Tickets please" he repeated "thank you" as each ticket was handed to him. "I shouldn't wake 'im up if I was you!" said Maggie "'e'll bite yer 'and off!" The ticket collector took a small step back, thought better of it and departed. "Good job 'ee didn't wake 'im weren' it Flo. Pass us anover of them sweets love, I'll buy some fer the return journey okey?". The train had stopped at Yovil for water and coal. There was a lot of shouting and chat from the driver and the station master. The sea gulls were screeching and the day was beautiful. The smell of ozone was strong though they were few miles from the coast was making the women heady with excitement now they were nearing Exeter.

Both Maggie and Flo were still laughing at the memory of that day in Southend, but still Flo didn't say anything, she was lost in her own thoughts of that day. It had been a lovely sunny day, if her memory served her right, and they had been on all those penny slot machines until their money had run out. A right nice looking fella had taken a shine to her, followed her all around too. Paid for the coconut shy then put his arm around her to help win a teddy bear – cheeky monkey. Then stole a kiss so quick she hadn't had time to object.

The sleeping man gave another snort. Maggie raised her eyebrows to dismiss it.

"I didn't see yer win that bear Flo you carried around all the time. Wouldn' let i' go even when we was on that big wheel thing! I fought yer didn' av anymore money! Do yer remember?" Maggie turned to face her friend "ow did you get it anyway? Yer never could throw a ball straigh' to save yer life could yer?"

Flo just smiled remembering. She had felt that fella's eyes on her all afternoon until just before they had to get back on the coach.

"ere Flo wha' do yer fink of tha' then?" beaming Maggie held up the finished front of the jumper "now fer the back. Coming on quick innit?" Maggie was beginning to enjoy making the jumper forgetting why she was so cross to start with.

Flo looked and smiled. The man back then had said she had a lovely smile then his hands had strayed to her bottom. She had given him a hard slap before running to catch Maggie up. It was real funny how she remembered different things to Maggie. She also remembered dipping their toes in the cold sea and running back to join the others laughing. It was the first time they'd seen the sea and loved the surf breaking over their toes and the sinking feeling as the sand seemed to fall away as the waves rushed back. She'd been back several times since then staying in the same boarding house year on year. She would sit in the window on rainy days and watch the people as they fought against the wind smiling to herself as they battled with their umbrellas and children. Flo had no children of her own but was an unofficial aunt to Maggie's three who she loved dearly.

Just then there was an announcement to tell them they were coming into Exeter Station.

"Come on Flo" Maggie was packing her knitting away while searching for the familiar face of

Daphne "there she is" suddenly noticing there was something very different about her "oh Flo she narf put on a lot of weight – it is Daphne innit?"

Both the women couldn't believe their friend was so big as she had been so tiny before, with open arms they all hugged each other "You're bigger 'an yer were Daph and 'ow are yer" Maggie was talking ten times to the dozen hardly taking a breath "where yer bin girl all this time?" and "wha' yer bin doing Daph love?"

Flo could see quite plainly what she'd been doing and how could she get herself up the duff at her age for goodness sake, she must be in her sixties if not more the same as them. And what's she done with her hair too? I'd die if it was me Flo thought, Oh the shame of it!

"Well yer see my Bill left me fer a young bit of stuff 'an we'd been married all them years too. Anyway I 'ad to get away didn't I you know somewhere differen' so I went on this 'oliday to Spain didn't I"

"Well" explained Daphne "I was on this 'oliday see and this fella was ever so nice ta me – and you can guess the rest" patting her oversized tummy "we got married too, then 'e scarpered didn' 'e as soon as we was off the plane more or less."

"Oh Daph how could you" and "the rotten so an' so. I'd like ta give him a piece of my mind I could tell yer, bloody cheek.." For once Maggie was practically speechless.

"yes and 'e took me fer all I had too" Daphne started to cry "'ow am I going to manage" tears were flowing now she had her friends to talk too "I must look a right fool. Yer see I'd gone over there ta get over me Rob leaving me fer this young thing – half 'is age too, so I was right pissed and knackered after a lovely nigh' out. He looked after me sor' of......" her voice trailed off amid sobs

"Don't say anover word Daph love, we get the picture. Yer ear of that now an then on the tele don' yer Flo? Didn't fink you would get caught though Daph love as yer always bin sor' of particalar 'aven't yer? Anyway we'll take care of yer woan' we Flo" Flo nodded her head rather too quickly as though it was one of those dogs some people buy for the rear windows of their cars "yer will 'ave to come back wiv us woan' she Flo?" Maggie put her arms protectively around her friend "no wonder yer didn' say anyfin before, but yer should 'ave let us know sooner Daph an' we couldof bin able ter help yer more." Both Maggie and Flo thought of the same thing at

154

the same time but didn't say anything for fear of upsetting their friend.

"How far yer gone then?" asked Maggie looking her up and doqn.

"Almost there - eight an' a half months. Oh Maggie what am I gonna do?" Daphne had started crying again.

"We'll go to yer place and pack a bag see, then we'll go back to the 'ol smoke an' see if we can sort somefin' out o'key?"

Maggie hailed a taxis, "come on let's go to yer place an' pick up yer bits 'an come back wiv us okey? Yer'll be alright wiv us.

Later the same day the three were on the train, this time though it was Maggie soothing Daphne with Flo nodding approval. No more knitting was done on the homeward journey. When they arrived at Maggie's house in Ford Street just opposite Victoria Park in the East End, she explained everything to Fred and after a nice cup of tea Fred produced a pamphlet and receipt for a weekend at a health farm Maggie had wanted to go to but never been able to afford.

"What yer got there then?" she asked him

"it's fer me lovey dove" he always called Maggie that "I spent yer money on yer instead of a 'oliday fer us. Is that alright darlin'?" Now it was Maggie who was crying.

"I love yer yer silly 'ol man, come ere an' give us a kiss."

Daphne had her baby girl and named her Maggie Flo after her two wonderful friends. She has masses of black hair and beautiful large eyes. Daphne had found a small flat in the same road as Maggie and soon had also started a small business making soft toys to sell in the little market at the end of the road. She didn't make much money but she was happier than she had ever been. They all remained friends and will do so till the end of their days. Little Maggie Flo grew up into a lovely young lady and always remembered her Mum, Aunt Maggie and Auntie Flo. When they needed help she was always on hand and later she became their carer. By then they were all living in a house together enjoying each other's company. When Maggie Flo married they simply bought a larger house then as two children arrived it was just one big happy family.